About this Learning Guide

Shmoop Will Make You a Better Lover*
*of Literature, History, Poetry, Life...

Our lively learning guides are written by experts and educators who want to show your brain a good time. Shmoop writers come primarily from Ph.D. programs at top universities, including Stanford, Harvard, and UC Berkeley.

Want more Shmoop? We cover literature, poetry, bestsellers, music, US history, civics, biographies (and the list keeps growing). Drop by our website to see the latest.

www.shmoop.com

Table of Contents

Introduction 3
    In a Nutshell 3
    Why Should I Care? 3
Summary 4
    Book Summary 4
    Part One 4
    Part Two 5
    Part Three 5
    Part Four 6
    Part Five 6
    Part Six, Woman in the Wallpaper 6
    Part Seven 6
    Part Eight, Woman in the Wallpaper 7
    Part Nine 7
    Part Ten 7
    Part Eleven 7
    Part Twelve 7
Themes 8
    Theme of Freedom and Confinement 8
    Questions About Freedom and Confinement 8
    Chew on Freedom and Confinement 8
    Theme of Madness 9
    Questions About Madness 9
    Chew on Madness 9
    Theme of Gender 9
    Questions About Gender 9
    Chew on Gender 10
    Theme of Literature and Writing 10
    Questions About Literature and Writing 10
    Chew on Literature and Writing 10
    Theme of Society and Class 10
    Questions About Society and Class 10
    Chew on Society and Class 11
Quotes 11
    Freedom and Confinement Quotes 11
    Madness Quotes 12
    Gender Quotes 13
    Literature and Writing Quotes 14
    Society and Class Quotes 15
Plot Analysis 16
    Classic Plot Analysis 16
    Three Act Plot Analysis 17
Study Questions 17

Characters 18
   All Characters 18
      The Narrator Character Analysis 18
      The Narrator Timeline and Summary 23
      John Character Analysis 24
      John Timeline and Summary 24
      The Woman in the Wallpaper Character Analysis 24
      Mary Character Analysis 27
      Jennie Character Analysis 28
   Character Roles 28
   Character Clues 28
Literary Devices 29
   Symbols, Imagery, Allegory 29
   Setting 30
   Narrator Point of View 31
   Genre 31
   Tone 31
   Writing Style 32
   What's Up With the Title? 32
   What's Up With the Ending? 32
Did You Know? 32
   Trivia 32
   Steaminess Rating 33
   Allusions and Cultural References 33
Best of the Web 33
   Movie or TV Productions 33
   Audios 34
   Images 34
   Documents 34
   Websites 34

Introduction

In a Nutshell

In 1887, Charlotte Perkins Gilman went to see a specialist in the hope of curing her recurring nervous breakdowns. The specialist recommended a "rest cure," which consisted of lying in bed all day and engaging in intellectual activity for only two hours a day. After three months, Gilman says, she was "near the borderline of utter mental ruin." (See "Why I Wrote the *Yellow Wallpaper*")

In due time, Gilman disregarded the specialist's advice and wrote "The Yellow Wallpaper" to demonstrate the kind of madness produced by the popular "rest cure." It was published in 1891 in *New England Magazine* . For the first decade of its life, "The Yellow Wallpaper" was read as a piece of horror fiction firmly situated in the Gothic genre. Since the 1960s, however, it has been anthologized as a piece of the women's movement illustrating 19th century attitudes towards women's physical and mental health. (See our discussion of "Genre" for more on this.) According to Gilman, the short story was never intended as a Gothic horror, but rather as a cautionary tale about what supposed "rest cures" could do to the mental stability of patients. In her own words, Gilman wrote: "It was not intended to drive people crazy, but to save people from being driven crazy, and it worked." She sent a copy to the physician who had recommended a rest cure, and he subsequently changed his medical practices.

Why Should I Care?

Remember how, when you were a kid and you were being maybe a little obnoxious and your parents sent you to your room or gave you a timeout? Remember when you had to sit still or stay inside, when all your friends were playing and you weren't allowed to join them, the time seemed to *streeeetch* on forever? Maybe your mind started to waver and wander, and perhaps you started to imagine, we don't know – something along the lines of the wallpaper in your room *coming alive*? There's a *reason* people in movies freak out in solitary confinement: having nothing to do for hours on end makes you a little nuts.

The thing is, Charlotte Perkins Gilman is counting on the fact that you, the reader, have at some time in your life been sent to bed without supper or been stuck inside when you wanted to go out. She's counting on the fact that you know something about claustrophobia or resentment so that you can sympathize with the narrator of this short story in her slow trajectory towards madness.

Gilman doesn't want to create some clinical study of insanity here; she wants you to *feel* every crawling inch of craziness. She knows you've got an imagination, that you can guess, from your experiences of a couple of hours of tedium, what a whole summer of solitary confinement would be like – and we're gambling that she's right. It's tough to read this story without wondering if, under similar circumstances circumstances, you yourself might start crawling out of the yellow wallpaper.

Maybe the specific injustices Gilman fights in this story – issues like men's excessive power over their wives and doctors' excessive power over their patients – seem like they belong more to the 1890s than to the current millennium. But we still read "The Yellow Wallpaper" even so, because the story's language is powerful enough to reach out of the page and make you feel like maybe *you're* cracking up. Gilman relies on the reader's own enduring (and often ugly) human feelings to give you a deeply disturbing snapshot of what *you* might be like after something as simple as a summer inside – and that snapshot is no pretty picture.

Summary

Book Summary

The narrator and her husband John are renting a beautiful, secluded estate for the summer. The narrator suffers from what her husband believes is a "temporary nervous depression." He orders her to rest as much as possible, and picks a room in the house for the two of them. The narrator feels vaguely uncomfortable with the estate, but obeys her husband's decision for the two of them to stay there. She also obeys him when he chooses a large, airy room on the top floor instead of the smaller, prettier room on the ground floor that she prefers. Since her husband is a doctor, he wins all their arguments. The narrator would like to spend her time writing, but her husband, brother, and assorted other family members think this is a terrible idea.

Let's recap: the narrator is living in a house in which she feels uncomfortable, in a room she hasn't picked out, and is forbidden from engaging in the one activity she enjoys. No wonder she becomes absolutely obsessed with the yellow wallpaper in her room. She begins fanatically tracing the pattern of the wallpaper and soon becomes convinced that there is a woman trapped within the paper. Shortly before the narrator is due to depart the house, she decides that she must free the trapped woman by stripping the wallpaper off. When her husband comes into the room, the narrator declares that she is now free. Upon seeing his wife creeping around the room peeling the paper off the walls, John faints. The narrator continues creeping around the room.

Part One

- The narrator and her husband John move into an old ancestral hall for the summer.
- She immediately feels that there is something wrong with the place, but John scoffs at her fears, which seems to be a recurring theme in their marriage. John uses the old, "trust me, I'm a doctor" line to convince his wife and all their relatives that the narrator needs to rest in order to get rid of her slight depression.
- The narrator thinks that writing and hanging out with friends would be a better cure, but Mr. "trust me, I'm a doctor" wins the day. The narrator occasionally sneaks around and writes, but it's hard when her husband and family oppose it.
- The narrator transitions to describing the estate as one of those "English places that you read about."
- The narrator continues feeling spooked out by the place, and John again dismisses her fears. She wants to sleep in a different, prettier room, but her husband disagrees. He

recommends a large room at the top of the house that used to be a nursery.

- John controls her daily schedule and prescribes lots and lots of rest. The narrator hates the wallpaper in the room, which is stripped off in various places.
- Even though she hates the wallpaper, the narrator is also strangely fascinated by it.
- She tells us that John is approaching and that she must hide the paper she is writing on.

Part Two

- Two weeks have passed.
- The narrator is too weak to do much writing. She complains of suffering and guilt-trips herself for being unable to fulfill her duties.
- A woman named Mary is taking care of the narrator's baby. The narrator says she is nervous around her own son.
- John almost gives in and repapers the room, but decides the narrator would then demand all sorts of other changes.
- The narrator says she is becoming fonder of the room, except for the horrible wallpaper.
- She gives us an overview of the view from her window.
- The narrator wishes she could spend time as a writer, but resolves not to think about it.
- She opts for describing the wallpaper instead. According to her, it is full of "absurd, unblinking eyes."
- All the furniture in the room is also beat up, which doesn't particularly bother the narrator.
- She hears Jennie, John's sister, on the stairs, who we learn is a perfect housekeeper, and the narrator is afraid to be caught writing.
- The narrator notes that the wallpaper has a sub-pattern to it, behind which she can see "a strange, provoking, formless sort of figure."
- She hears John's sister on the stairs.

Part Three

- The Fourth of July has passed. The narrator has had some company, but now she is tired.
- John threatens to send her to Weir Mitchell if she doesn't get better, but she doesn't want that – she's had friends treated by the man and apparently he's just like John.
- Her mind grows more chaotic as she begins randomly crying.
- She stays alone in her room or walks in the garden.
- She grows more obsessed with the wallpaper and is determined to find a purpose to the pattern.
- It tires her out and she decides to take a nap.

Part Four

- The narrator continues to lose her willpower and strength. She tries to talk reasonably to her husband about visiting her relatives, but breaks down and starts crying during the conversation.
- John tells her she must take care of herself for his sake.
- The narrator continues to watch the wallpaper. Within the pattern, the shape of a woman creeping is becoming clearer.
- The narrator wishes she could leave.

Part Five

- The narrator watches the wallpaper in the moonlight and can see the woman trying to break free of the paper.
- She gets out of bed to look more closely. Her husband wakes up and calls her back to bed. She asks to leave the estate and he tells her that they cannot leave.
- He then assures her that she's getting better, using the "trust me, I'm a doctor" rationale.
- He goes back to sleep and the narrator stays up watching the pattern.

Part Six, Woman in the Wallpaper

- The narrator continues to describe the pattern, calling it a bad dream.
- By moonlight the pattern looks different to the narrator.
- The narrator is now convinced that, trapped in the wallpaper, there is a woman, who remains very still during the day.
- The narrator spends all her time in bed, and she begins to fear both John and his sister Jennie. She is convinced they are somehow also connected to the paper.
- Convinced that Jennie has also begun studying the wallpaper, the narrator is determined to uncover its secret herself.

Part Seven

- Life becomes more exciting for the narrator as she grows more obsessed with the wallpaper.
- She keeps her obsession to herself. She doesn't want John to find out.
- We learn the narrator will be in the house for only one more week.

Part Eight, Woman in the Wallpaper

- The narrator feels better. She is now sleeping during the day and lies awake at night watching the wallpaper.
- She says there are always interesting developments. Now the wallpaper smells.
- She describes it as the color of the wallpaper, a "yellow smell."
- She notes a funny streak that runs the length of the room.

Part Nine

- The narrator believes she has made a breakthrough. She believes the front pattern of the wallpaper moves because the woman trapped behind it is shaking it.
- The narrator thinks the woman is trying to escape, but the pattern of the wallpaper is strangling her. This, thinks the narrator, explains all the heads and the bulging eyes.

Part Ten

- The narrator is convinced that the woman escapes during the daytime.
- The narrator says she sees the woman creeping along the road, and that most women don't creep by daylight.
- We find out that the narrator has been creeping by daylight – she just locks the door. She knows her husband would catch her if she were to creep around at night.
- The narrator continues to watch the other woman creep.

Part Eleven

- The narrator has two days left. She's trying to remove the top pattern of the wallpaper.
- She is convinced John and Jennie are conspiring against her.
- She is convinced John and Jennie have been affected by the wallpaper.

Part Twelve

- It's the last day in the house.
- John stays in town overnight with a patient, and Jennie offers to keep the narrator company, but she declines.
- As soon as night falls, the narrator goes to the wallpaper to help the woman trapped inside.
- The narrator and the trapped woman peel away yards of the wallpaper.

- The sun rises and the narrator believes the pattern is laughing at her.
- She is due to leave tomorrow with John.
- Jennie comes into the room and is astounded to see much of the wallpaper gone.
- The narrator says she will sleep the rest of the day and requests that no one disturb her.
- After Jennie leaves, the narrator locks the door, throws the key down the stairs, and gets to work. The narrator prepares a rope to capture the woman in the wallpaper once she gets out.
- The narrator then tries to move the bed so she can stand on it to strip the wallpaper.
- The bed doesn't move. The narrator gets so enraged that she bites it.
- She gets angry enough that she contemplates jumping out the window, only to find that the windows are barred.
- The narrator is happy that she can now creep around the room as she wishes.
- John tries to get in the room.
- He pounds on the door and the narrator finally tells him that the key is on the front path.
- He comes in and is shocked to see his wife creeping about.
- The narrator tells John that she (the narrator) has finally escaped and that he cannot put her back.
- John faints as the narrator continues to creep around the room.

Themes

Theme of Freedom and Confinement

The narrator in "The Yellow Wallpaper" is essentially confined to a single room in a large house. Conversely, her husband frequently spends his nights in town as part of his duties as a bigshot doctor. This dichotomy is the overwhelmingly dominant theme of the story, as the narrator's attempts to cope with isolation wind up being the engine driving the plot forward.

Questions About Freedom and Confinement

1. Is the narrator truly liberated at the end of the story? Why or why not?
2. Who is responsible for the narrator's confinement? How can you tell?
3. To what extent is the narrator responsible for her own confinement?
4. To what extent is the narrator aware of her own imprisonment?

Chew on Freedom and Confinement

The narrator is not liberated at the end of the story. Rather, she has simply fallen deeply into mental illness.

The narrator has successfully liberated herself by the end of the story.

Theme of Madness

Due to the narrator's confinement, she begins losing her sanity. Most importantly for this story, we see the narrator's descent into madness through her eyes. Readers stay with the narrator as her mind grows more chaotic and as she begins seeing shapes in the wallpaper. This is the ultimate example of showing, not telling. We have to deduce from her frantic writing style that there isn't *actually* a woman trapped in the wallpaper; the narrator just thinks there is because she's losing her grip on reality.

Questions About Madness

1. At what point in the story has the narrator truly descended into madness?
2. When is the narrator considered mentally ill by her husband and incapable of making her own decisions? Does this intersect with your answer to the first question at all? How does being considered insane interact with actual point of madness in this story?
3. Why does the narrator become mentally ill?

Chew on Madness

In "The Yellow Wallpaper," the narrator's rich imagination might have found a productive and healthy outlet in her writing, but being forced to repress her imagination instead leads her to madness.

Theme of Gender

The reason for the narrator's confinement is her gender. Although explicit references to either gender in the text are rare, there is certainly a gendered subtext, especially given what we know about the period in which Gilman was writing (late 1800s). The narrator's confinement and repression are strictly based on her gender. The women we see in the story are meant to find fulfillment in the home, while the men hold positions as high-ranking physicians. The narrator's lack of a name also reinforces the notion that she is speaking as the voice of women collectively, rather than as an individual.

Questions About Gender

1. To what extent does the narrator articulate the position and experience of womanhood at large? (Hint: think about women of color, poor women, etc.)
2. How are women represented in the story? What about men? What positions does each gender hold in terms of occupation, power, etc.?
3. Are there aspects of the narrator's story that are still legitimate critiques of today's gender relations?

Chew on Gender

Although women today are no longer prescribed "rest cures," the broader concept of women being imprisoned by societal mores remains a highly relevant concept.

"The Yellow Wallpaper" critiques only the life of wealthy white women and excludes the plight of low-income and women of color.

Theme of Literature and Writing

In "The Yellow Wallpaper," writing is a healthy means of self-actualization denied to the narrator. The narrator portrays writing positively in the story, believing that it will help her depression. Others around her, however, heavily disapprove of her writing, believing it to be a tiring activity.

Questions About Literature and Writing

1. Can you read the text as a personal diary? How does this reading affect the way you interpret the story?
2. What is the narrator's attitude towards her writing? What are other people's attitudes towards her writing?
3. Is there a connection between the narrator's writing and the idea that she is *reading* the paper on the wall?

Chew on Literature and Writing

In "The Yellow Wallpaper," the narrator's rich imagination might have found a productive and healthy outlet in her writing, but being forced to repress her imagination instead leads her to madness.

Theme of Society and Class

The story and message of "The Yellow Wallpaper" are rooted in a very specific class and societal dynamic. The narrator is a member of the upper class; she and her husband are wealthy enough to take a summer off and have servants cater to their every need. In this fashion, the narrator's story may be critiqued for limiting itself to the troubles of *wealthy* women. The society described in "The Yellow Wallpaper" concerns not only a certain class, but also a certain type of society, in which women play limited roles.

Questions About Society and Class

1. Are there aspects of the narrator's story that are particularly class-based? Which? Remember that work is not a necessity for her. Are there aspects of her story that are timeless and apply to all women, regardless of class or race?
2. What is the effect of the narrator identifying herself and her husband as "mere ordinary people"?
3. To what extent is the narrator conscious of her own place in society?

Chew on Society and Class

Working-class women can identify with the narrator's story of women's oppression by men.

Working-class women may have trouble identifying with "The Yellow Wallpaper" because the narrator's story deals very specifically with the problems experienced by women of the upper class.

Quotes

Freedom and Confinement Quotes

He said that after the wall-paper was changed it would be the heavy bedstead, and then the barred windows, and then that gate at the head of the stairs, and so on. (1.14)

Thought: The heavy bedstead (or bed frame), barred windows, and gate at the head of the stairs all provide a physical confinement that mirrors the narrator's societal confinement.

There are hedges and walls and gates that lock, and lots of separate little houses for the gardeners and people. (1.19)

Thought: The structure of the house itself highlights the narrator's confinement.

John is away all day, and even some nights when his cases are serious. (2.3)

Thought: While the narrator must remain at home, essentially confined to her bedroom, John is free to go out and about.

At night in any kind of light, in twilight, candlelight, lamplight, and worst of all by moonlight, it becomes bars! The outside pattern I mean, and the woman behind it is as plain as can be. (6.10)

Thought: As the narrator later identifies with the woman trapped in the wallpaper, we understand that her subconscious is more aware of her imprisonment than her conscious mind, which continues to believe that John wants the best for her.

Sometimes I think there are a great many women behind, and sometimes only one, and she crawls around fast, and her crawling shakes it all over. [...]

And she is all the time trying to climb through. But nobody could climb through that pattern--it strangles so; I think that is why it has so many heads. (9.4 – 9.6)

Thought: This passage demonstrates the intersection of confinement and gender – the narrator sometimes sees many, many women imprisoned by the pattern.

"I've got out at last," said I, "in spite of you and Jane. And I've pulled off most of the paper, so you can't put me back!" (12.49)

Thought: Notice how she identifies herself with the trapped woman in the wallpaper. The narrator believes that she has freed herself. What do you think? Is this really freedom? Also, see "Names" in "Tools of Characterization" for a discussion of who this Jane character might be.

Madness Quotes

I always fancy I see people walking in these numerous paths and arbors, but John has cautioned me not to give way to fancy in the least. He says that with my imaginative power and habit of story-making, a nervous weakness like mine is sure to lead to all manner of excited fancies, and that I ought to use my will and good sense to check the tendency. So I try.

I think sometimes that if I were only well enough to write a little it would relieve the press of ideas and rest me. (2.22 – 2.23)

Thought: John forces the narrator to repress her imagination. While her "habit of story-making" might have found a healthy outlet in writing, repression of her habit instead damages the narrator.

I never saw so much expression in an inanimate thing before, and we all know how much expression they have! I used to lie awake as a child and get more entertainment and terror out of blank walls and plain furniture than most children could find in a toy-store. (2.70)

Thought: Since her husband repeatedly treats her like a child, the narrator begins reverting to childlike fancies.

"Better in body perhaps--" I began, and stopped short, for he sat up straight and looked at me with such a stern, reproachful look that I could not say another word. "My darling," said he, "I beg of you, for my sake and for our child's sake, as well as for your own, that you will never for one instant let that idea enter your mind! There is nothing so dangerous, so fascinating, to a temperament like yours. It is a false and foolish fancy. Can you not trust me as a physician when I tell you so?" (5.16 – 5.17)

Thought: When she expresses her own opinions, John treats the narrator as though she were crazy. This leads to actual mental illness.

On a pattern like this, by daylight, there is a lack of sequence, a defiance of law, that is a constant irritant to a normal mind. (6.1)

Thought: Since her mind has nothing else in the world to focus on, the narrator is driven to an obsession with the wallpaper. Here she is still in her normal mind (or is she?), but her brain – for lack of any other occupation – soon fixates on the wallpaper to an unhealthy degree.

Life is very much more exciting now than it used to be. You see I have something more to expect, to look forward to, to watch. I really do eat better, and am more quiet than I was. (7.1)

Thought: This is arguably the moment in the story at which the narrator has truly lost her sanity.

"I've got out at last," said I, "in spite of you and Jane. And I've pulled off most of the paper, so you can't put me back!" (12.49)

Thought: The narrator believes that she is liberated, but at this point, she has also lost her sanity. Can we trust what she says?

Gender Quotes

My brother is also a physician, and also of high standing, and he says the same thing. (1.11)

Thought: The men in the narrator's life have prestigious, active jobs and their opinions dictate the way she lives her life.

[Jennie] is a perfect and enthusiastic housekeeper, and hopes for no better profession. I verily believe she thinks it is the writing which made me sick! (2.77)

Thought: John's sister Jennie embodies the ideal woman of this age.

Sometimes I think there are a great many women behind, and sometimes only one, and she crawls around fast, and her crawling shakes it all over. [...]

And she is all the time trying to climb through. But nobody could climb through that pattern--it strangles so; I think that is why it has so many heads. (9.4 – 9.6)

Thought: This is a passage demonstrating the intersection of confinement and gender – the narrator sometimes sees many, many women imprisoned by the pattern.

It is the same woman, I know, for she is always creeping, and most women do not creep by daylight. (10.4)

Thought: This implies that the narrator believes *all* women creep at night.

Literature and Writing Quotes

Personally, I believe that congenial work, with excitement and change, would do me good. (1.14)

Thought: Literature in "The Yellow Wallpaper" is the healthiest means of self-actualization.

I did write for a while in spite of them; but it does exhaust me a good deal--having to be so sly about it, or else meet with heavy opposition.

I sometimes fancy that in my condition if I had less opposition and more society and stimulus--but John says the very worst thing I can do is to think about my condition, and I confess it always makes me feel bad. (1.17 – 1.18)

Thought: Everyone around the narrator opposes her desire to write, which, as you might imagine, makes writing rather difficult.

We have been here two weeks, and I haven't felt like writing before, since that first day.

I am sitting by the window now, up in this atrocious nursery, and there is nothing to hinder my writing as much as I please, save lack of strength. (2.1 – 2.2)

Thought: The narrator has been drained of her desire to write because of the persistent opposition of the people around her.

I always fancy I see people walking in these numerous paths and arbors, but John has cautioned me not to give way to fancy in the least. He says that with my imaginative power and habit of story-making, a nervous weakness like mine is sure to lead to all manner of excited fancies, and that I ought to use my will and good sense to check the tendency. So I try.

I think sometimes that if I were only well enough to write a little it would relieve the press of ideas and rest me. (2.22 – 2.23)

Thought: John forces the narrator to repress her imagination. While her "habit of story-making" might have found a healthy outlet in writing, repressing her habit instead leads to the narrator's mental illness.

I think sometimes that if I were only well enough to write a little it would relieve the press of ideas and rest me.

But I find I get pretty tired when I try.

It is so discouraging not to have any advice and companionship about my work. When I get really well, John says we will ask Cousin Henry and Julia down for a long visit; but he says he would as soon put fireworks in my pillow-case as to let me have those stimulating people about now. (2.23 – 2.25)

Thought: Here John is a clear obstacle to the narrator's desire to write and to lead an engaged, fulfilling life.

[Jennie] is a perfect and enthusiastic housekeeper, and hopes for no better profession. I verily believe she thinks it is the writing which made me sick! (2.77)

Thought: Jennie's belief is characteristic of the perfect "angel in the house" ideal.

Society and Class Quotes

It is very seldom that mere ordinary people like John and myself secure ancestral halls for the summer. (1.1)

Thought: The narrator thinks of herself and her husband as "ordinary people." How accurate is that? Remember that they have servants, including a housekeeper *and* a nanny.

If a physician of high standing, and one's own husband, assures friends and relatives that there is really nothing the matter with one but temporary nervous depression--a slight hysterical tendency-- what is one to do? (1.10)

Thought: Here, John's status in society as a doctor and a husband both conspire against the narrator's articulation of her own illness.

I sometimes fancy that in my condition if I had less opposition and more society and stimulus--but John says the very worst thing I can do is to think about my condition, and I confess it always makes me feel bad. (1.17)

Thought: The narrator is cut off and isolated from the rest of the society. Is that the real source of her madness?

The faint figure behind seemed to shake the pattern, just as if she wanted to get out. (5.6)

Thought: Everyone can identify with wanting to shake loose the strictures of society.

Plot Analysis

Classic Plot Analysis

Initial Situation
The narrator feels uneasy on the estate she and her husband have rented for the summer.
Do you sense the beginning of a horror story? We do: a woman moves into the house; the house is spooky; the woman has serious misgivings; etc. We also learn in this stage that the narrator's husband makes all the decisions for her, telling her when she is sick and what she is suffering from. This is part of the initial situation as it highlights a certain path that the story may follow.

Conflict
The narrator wishes to spend her time writing and socializing, but her husband tells her she must rest.
The narrator tries to express her own opinion to her husband, but is overruled on every count. This is conflict, yes, but note its one-sided nature: John doesn't take his wife seriously. In other words, this conflict results in the narrator's repression.

Complication
The wallpaper freaks out the narrator, and she imagines a woman trapped within the paper.
Forced to lie in bed all day and rest, the narrator becomes completely entranced by the wallpaper and is drawn into trying to decode its design. This adds a layer of complication to the story as the narrator's vibrant mind deals with repression by focusing on her surroundings.

Climax
The narrator strips off all the wallpaper in her room.
This is the ultimate moment of rebellion for the protagonist as she takes action towards freedom. She is finally upsetting the status quo and declaring her own sense of agency. This all adds up to one heck of a climactic moment.

Suspense
John attempts to find out what his wife is up to.
All of this upsetting of the status quo comes with a certain amount of backlash. When John comes home to find the door to his bedroom locked, he begins freaking out. The uncertainty of the narrator's fate leads us to conclude that this is the moment of suspense.

Denouement
John faints.

The narrator's actions are so extraordinary and so shocking that her husband faints. This is the denouement because it answers our questions about how John will react to his wife's craziness. Rather than bullying her or trying to talk to her, he simply faints.

Conclusion

The narrator continues to strip off the wallpaper, convinced that she has achieved liberation at last.

This is the conclusion of the story because it's how we leave the scene of the story. It functions a bit oddly as a conclusion, however, because it doesn't exactly wrap up loose ends. For instance, we're wondering if the narrator ever gets her sanity back. Does her husband regain consciousness? Does she get tired of creeping? Wait a minute. This doesn't seem like a conclusion at all!

Three Act Plot Analysis

Act I

The narrator and her husband arrive at a country estate for a "rest" vacation. She is bothered by their room's ugly yellow wallpaper.

Act II

Stuck in the room with orders to do nothing but rest, the narrator becomes more obsessed with the wallpaper and less trusting of her husband. She begins to sense a "yellow smell" in the room.

Act III

Convinced there's a woman stuck behind the wallpaper, she strips it off the walls in order to free her. She then declares that she has escaped from the paper, and her husband faints when he finally sees how insane she has become.

Study Questions

1. What would "The Yellow Wallpaper" look like as a full-length novel? Why do you think it's presented in the short story form instead?
2. To what extent is the narrator reliable?
3. How is the story broken down into different sections? Do you think there are other effective divisions within the story?
4. How do you know the narrator is a woman?
5. Is the narrator's name "Jane"? (See our discussion of Names in "Tools of Characterization.")
6. What are some of the problems with reading "The Yellow Wallpaper" as a feminist text? For instance, does the narrator speak for all women? Could the men in the story also be understood as repressed individuals?

7. Does the story belong more to the Gothic horror genre or the feminist literary fiction genre?
8. Does the ending of the story suggest progress (a woman tears down the shackles that are binding her) or pessimism (this woman has become completely unstable)? Or is it delivering a different type of message? How should we read this story?

Characters

All Characters

The Narrator Character Analysis

Introducing...Jane Doe

The first line of "The Yellow Wallpaper" does double duty, introducing both the setting of the story – a home for someone else's ancestors – and the story's narrator: "It is very seldom that mere ordinary people like John and myself secure ancestral homes for the summer" (3).

We know that the narrator is 1) a woman (because she is married to a man, and this is 1890), 2) probably middle class ("mere ordinary people"), and 3) has a husband named John. All of this is actually pretty aggressively anonymous: the narrator has no name and is married to a guy who might as well have no name, since "John" doesn't really give us any clues about who he is or where he might be from.

The fact that these three traits – her gender, her class, and her marriage – all make it into the first sentence (while her name doesn't) suggests that these general characteristics may be more important to the unfolding of the plot than her actual identity or personal history (about which we learn very little).

Why are these traits so important? Because they provide the context central conflicts that drive the story. The narrator is a woman of sensitive temperament, and she is also a writer. She has been ill, and her illness has placed her in a weak position in relation to domineering John. As her husband *and* as her physician (a situation we think the American Medical Association would find problematic), John makes all of the narrator's decisions for her, which really irritates her:

If a physician of high standing, and one's own husband, assures friends and relatives that there is really nothing the matter with one but temporary nervous depression – a slight hysterical tendency – what is one to do? (3)

So, "one's own husband" is badmouthing the narrator to her friends and refusing to take her seriously. That might have us crawling up the walls, too.

And what about class? Well, our Jane Doe apparently is of a social position that means she doesn't have to work. She may be middle class enough that staying at an ancestral home is a new thing for her, but she's still definitely on the upper end of the social spectrum. Maybe this lack of labor would be lucky for her if she was allowed to do *anything else*, but her illness has restricted her activities pretty much entirely.

John has prescribed absolute rest – he won't even let her look after her baby. And while his intentions may be good, he's driving the narrator nuts from boredom. How do we know this? She tells us so within the first page: "I did write for a while in spite of [John telling me not too]; but it *does* exhaust me a good deal – having to be so sly about it, or else meet with heavy opposition." (3-4) The writing that she actively enjoys has been forbidden, so she has to do it in secret, leaving her tired and wrung out.

There's a binary between John (professional man) and our narrator (unemployed woman); there's also one between our narrator (lady of leisure) and her sister-in-law, Jennie (who takes care of the housework and the baby). Jennie may not have much power in the household, but she does have one thing that the narrator envies: an occupation.

There comes John's sister. Such a dear girl as she is, and so careful of me! I must not let her find me writing.

She is a perfect and enthusiastic housekeeper, and hopes for no better profession. I verily believe she thinks it is the writing which made me sick! (8)

Jennie's housekeeping gives her an authority over the narrator (who is, after all, doing zilch for anyone) that makes the narrator feel self-conscious and suspicious of Jennie's motives. As the story goes on, the narrator grows to resent John and Jennie more and more. With nothing to do but brood over how she has been wronged – and how incredibly ugly her wallpaper is – the narrator's paranoia has a field day.

Something else we can't help but notice in these previous passages: neither John nor Jennie thinks much of the activity of writing. They identify it as another symptom of the narrator's nervousness, her emotionality. But the narrator rebels against them without much fanfare right from the beginning, simply by stealing time to write "The Yellow Wallpaper."

The narrator's mental health hinges not only on *whether* she has work to do, but *what kind* of work it is. She wants to write and isn't allowed, something that " *does* exhaust her a good deal" (3). The subtle undermining of her confidence as a writer doesn't exactly help to repair the damaged relationships she shares with her husband and her sister-in-law, sending her further into a frenzy of paranoia that leads to her mounting obsession with the design of the paper on her bedroom wall.

So – Just *What* Is Wrong With Her?
Well, "The Yellow Wallpaper" remains as ambiguous and unclear about the narrator's illness as it does about her identity, so it's tough to say what, exactly, is wrong with her. Still, we know mental illness is going to be an issue right from the first page because, once again, the narrator

lets us know explicitly:

You see [John, the narrator's husband] does not believe I am sick! And what can one do? [...]

So I take phosphates or phosphites – whichever it is, and tonics, and journeys, and air, and exercise, and am absolutely forbidden to "work" until I am well again.

Personally, I disagree with [John and her physician brother's] ideas.

Personally, I believe that congenial work, with excitement and change, would do me good.

But what is one to do? (3)

We can get a lot about the character from this passage: first, she's pretty alienated from her own treatment ("phosphates or phosphites – whichever it is"? In our experience, anyone who really believes in the medicine she's taking isn't going to *forget what it's called*). Also, the antagonism between the narrator and pretty much everyone around her becomes apparent when she's all, " *Personally*, I disagree!"

Second, the narrator feels ill, but her ailment doesn't manifest physically. This is definitely an ongoing tension (as though their marriage *needed* more baggage) between the narrator and her physician husband, who "scoffs openly at any talk of things not to be felt and seen and put down in figures" (3).

Whenever the narrator tells John that she feels worse and worse, all he replies is that her body is getting better and better (though, why it was weak in the first place, we don't know. Perhaps her baby had a difficult birth?). He refuses to acknowledge that her mind could be sick even though her body is healthy.

We know from the outset that the narrator resents her husband's treatment and continues to feel unsettled even as she recovers physically. So, she's not starting the story in a great place mentally; the yellow wallpaper isn't so ugly that it can drive totally sane people out of their minds. But – our narrator isn't totally sane.

The story does a great job of suggesting the claustrophobic conditions that make her condition worse: note that the bed in her terrible attic room is *nailed down*, underlining how trapped the narrator is. She's not allowed to do anything that might "upset" her – in other words, that might give her release for her emotions: she's not allowed to write, she's not allowed to work, and she's not allowed to travel. (Is anyone else reminded of Nurse Ratched's treatments in *One Flew Over the Cuckoo's Nest* ? And look how *that* turned out.)

The only thing that the narrator has left to do is to speculate about the ugly, irregular wallpaper of the attic room. As she loses stability, the wallpaper's importance to her as the one puzzle she has to occupy herself with becomes greater and greater.

In fact, as she grows more certain that she *gets* the wallpaper as no one else does, the people she knows become correspondingly less understandable. Without any outlet beyond the

wallpaper, the narrator's anger builds, leading her to increasingly paranoid speculations about John and Jennie: "The fact is I am getting a little afraid of John. He seems very queer sometimes, and even Jennie has an inexplicable look" (13).

As she slowly aligns herself with the wallpaper and distances herself from John and Jennie, the narrator starts to recognize another woman creeping behind the pattern of the paper – and it's then that everything really hits the fan. For more on the creeping woman and the narrator's final breakdown, see the Woman in the Wallpaper "Character Analysis."

A Society Lady

So, let's talk for a second about this building obsession that drives our narrator to "get to work" (17) peeling away at the walls imprisoning a woman she sees behind the yellow wallpaper's maddening pattern. There is a moment, right at the end there, when the narrator slips into the persona of this creeping paper woman:

I don't like to look out of the windows even – there are so many of those creeping women, and they creep so fast.

I wonder if they all come out of that wallpaper as I did?

But I am securely fastened now by my well-hidden rope – you don't get me out in the road there!

I suppose I shall have to get back behind the pattern when it comes night, and that is hard!

It is so pleasant to be out in this great room and creep around as I please! (18)

Do you notice anything weird about this passage (besides – the obvious)? The narrator now believes that she is a woman recently freed from behind the bars of an ugly wallpaper pattern. But she's still talking (despite the exclamation points) like a well-bred society lady. Where's the cursing? How is she still making any kind of sense?

In a lot of ways, "The Yellow Wallpaper" reads like a real Gothic novel – oppressive husband, unfair social restrictions, a crazy lady – but the narrator, even in the depths of her breakdown, still writes like Edith Wharton.

Compare this to, say, that famous madwoman in the attic, Bertha in Charlotte Bronte's *Jane Eyre*, whose insanity makes her unable to speak. The narrator of this story, by contrast, is not only still totally verbally skilled, but remember – she's *writing about her own breakdown*. It's like the narrator has been so indoctrinated by social codes of the day that, even in the midst of a complete mental collapse, she still remembers to keep her journal and to be polite, both to herself and to poor, fainting John.

There's a logical progression to this story that doesn't surrender to the total mental breakdown of its heroine. This tips us off that "The Yellow Wallpaper," again, may be less interested in the particulars of its protagonist's mental state and more interested in protesting larger social issues like unjust treatment of the mentally ill and of women.

A Narrator We Can Believe In?

It may not seem like an obvious choice to end our character analysis by asking whether the person in question *is*, in fact, a character, but in the case of the nameless narrator of "The Yellow Wallpaper" it's worth thinking about. Because the narrator isn't just a character, she's also a plot device: for all of her apparent passivity, she really dominates the story, carefully sculpting not only what we know about her, but also what we *think* of her.

Lots of novels (check out Shmoop on *Moby Dick* or *The Great Gatsby* for examples) use the limited perspective of one marginal character to narrate (and make sense of) the (usually more exciting) people around him. It's a two for one deal. Not only do we, the readers, see the crazy shenanigans of a charismatic central character, like *Moby Dick*'s Captain Ahab or *The Great Gatsby*'s Jay Gatsby, but we *also* get one peripheral character (Ishmael in *Moby Dick*, Nick in *Gatsby*) telling us what he *thinks* of said shenanigans.

"The Yellow Wallpaper," though, offers pretty much no outside perspective on the actions of the story's heroine. It's like – if Bob Costas, instead of sitting at NBC commenting on, say, gymnast Shawn Johnson's performance at a competition, suddenly decided to put on a red leotard and jump on the balance beam himself. And after balancing his heart out, he wouldn't stop there, oh no! *Then* he'd move to the judge's bench and decide his own scores. Like imaginary Gymnast Bob, the narrator of "The Yellow Wallpaper" isn't just the story's main actor; she also provides all the background information and analysis made available to the reader.

Consolidating the narrator and the central character into one person is a really high-stakes way to tell a story. Why? Well, to return to Gymnast Bob, would *you* trust the opinion of someone who evaluated his own performance, without anyone to support his claims? The rewards are just as great as the risks, though: we tend to believe first person narrators (because, after all, we have nothing to go on but what they give us), and they have a lot of power over the reader's interpretation of events.

Let's take a look at some quotes from the narrator about her husband John to see the subtle way she shapes the reader's feelings about the people in her life.

1. *John laughs at me, of course, but one expects that in a marriage. (3)*
2. *I sometimes fancy that in my condition if I had less opposition and more society and stimulus—but John says the very worst thing I can do is to think about my condition, and I confess it always makes me feel bad. (4)*
3. *Dear John! He loves me very dearly, and hates to have me sick. I tried to have a real earnest reasonable talk with him the other day, and tell him how I wish he would let me go and make a visit to Cousin Henry and Julia.*

   But he said I wasn't able to go, nor able to stand it after I got there; and I did not make out a very good case for myself, for I was crying before I had finished. (10)

We know, from these passages, that 1) the narrator and John have frequent disagreements over her condition, 2) John doesn't take her seriously, and 3) their arguments make the

narrator cry.

The narrator's powerlessness, emotional distress, and pleas to John that she needs to get away – all of these make us sympathize with her, as does her effort to convince herself (and the reader) that she still loves the man in spite of his treatment of her. ("Dear John"? Come on.) John comes across as a big ol' jerk for not believing his wife when she tells him she's still feeling bad.

And *that's* the genius of the narration of "The Yellow Wallpaper": it seems natural, even inevitable, that we believe John's a horrible person, but who's telling us so? His discontented, desperately unhappy wife. And we're not saying you shouldn't believe her – John seems like an utter tool – but we do want to point out that it is also strategic, in a story challenging contemporary mental health treatment, to make the ailing narrator a total victim and the husband/doctor kind of a monster.

The Narrator Timeline and Summary

- The narrator and John arrive at an "ancestral home."
- John selects the large attic room for them to sleep in, which is papered with a really ugly yellow pattern the narrator hates.
- The narrator isn't allowed to write, do housework, or help with her baby.
- She begs John to be allowed to move elsewhere or to change rooms, because the inactivity is making her nervous and unhappy. John says no.
- Some people come to visit for the Fourth of July, leaving the narrator exhausted and fretful.
- She begins obsessively to try to follow the pattern of the wallpaper, to find some sort of logic or secret that would make it *make sense*.
- The narrator's fascination with the wallpaper mounts as she identifies a woman in the pattern, creeping behind the bars of the paper's design.
- The narrator asks John again to be allowed to visit his cousins or to move, and he again refuses, claiming that she's putting on weight and getting better.
- She begins to suspect that John and Jennie are also hiding secret obsessions with the wallpaper, and she resolves to figure it out *first*.
- The narrator's mood improves as she finds more and more sympathy for the woman trapped in the paper, particularly when she starts to see the creeping woman elsewhere in the house and outside (during the daylight).
- The narrator and John are on the verge of departing their summer home when the narrator locks herself in the attic and throws away the key.
- She seizes the opportunity to tear down huge chunks of the yellow wallpaper.
- In doing this, the narrator begins to assume the persona of the creeping woman.
- John, finally realizing how serious his wife's mental condition really is, breaks down the door. He sees her crawling on the floor, following the pattern of the paper, and faints.
- The creeping woman/narrator gets a little annoyed with John, since his unconscious body is blocking her view of the paper, and she has to crawl over him as she creeps around the room.

John Character Analysis

John is a high-ranking physician who tells his wife that he only wants the best for her; but he makes every decision regarding her life, right down to whom she gets to hang out with and to where she gets to sleep. The narrator writes that her husband John is "practical in the extreme." According to her, "He has no patience with faith, an intense horror of superstition, and he scoffs openly at any talk of things not to be felt and seen and put down in figures." As such, John embodies a supreme rationality that makes it difficult for the narrator to convince him of her sincere discomfort with her bedroom and the shapes that she sees within the wallpaper.

Although not the protagonist of the story, John is in some respects its central figure. First of all, he has an actual name, whereas the narrator is defined only in relation to her husband. (See "Tools of Characterization" for more on this.) John's decisions and opinions occupy most of the text as the narrator defers to his wishes. His character, moreover, is a great example of how the supposedly objective practice of science can actually be a gendered endeavor. Only his opinions count, for instance, when it comes to diagnosing the narrator's illness. While the rest cure may today seem like pseudo-science, in the 19th century it was a widely accepted and popular form of treatment for women with depression. In "The Yellow Wallpaper," Gilman tried to knock down these gendered and mistaken notions. Perhaps this is why John literally keels over in the story's final scene.

John Timeline and Summary

- John tells his wife that she suffers from a "temporary nervous depression."
- He dismisses his wife's sense of unease in the house and tells her to rest. A lot.
- John is very busy seeing patients in the city.
- John tells his wife that she is improving.
- He makes preparations for them to move out.
- John comes back home to find his wife peeling off the wallpaper in their room.
- He faints.

The Woman in the Wallpaper Character Analysis

We considered this one for a long time: is the woman behind the wallpaper, a woman whom our narrator is probably imagining, really a *character*? Our thinking is: the narrator comes to think of the woman behind the wallpaper as a separate woman, and since the narrator is telling us the story, we're willing to take the woman behind the wallpaper on the narrator's terms (at least, to start).

So, when does this woman emerge, and what characteristics does she have? Obviously, she's

strongly entwined with the narrator, so this analysis is also, in some ways, going to be an extended look at the narrator herself, and at the narrator's madness. But pretty much nothing in "The Yellow Wallpaper" *isn't* about the narrator, so we can't avoid coming back to her.

Let's begin with the wallpaper from whence the creeping woman comes. If the title — "The Yellow Wallpaper" — doesn't tip you off that the wallpaper is going to be a central factor in the story, the narrator's lengthy paragraphs of description should convince you. The paper's pattern is both "dull enough to confuse the eye in following" and "pronounced enough to constantly irritate" (5); the color is "repellant, almost revolting" (5). The wallpaper traps the narrator's attention by being simultaneously too irregular to ignore and too ugly to enjoy.

In a weird way, the wallpaper has human characteristics right from the start, because it's acting as a kind of foil for John: if the wallpaper traps the narrator's mind, John confines her physically. The inverse relationship between the two begins with the introduction of the wallpaper, when the narrator comments: "There comes John, and I must put this away, – he hates to have me write a word" (5). John's refusal to give the narrator anything to do drives her to the wallpaper for some kind of intellectual activity — even exhausting, damaging activity.

The narrator's ongoing, oddly passive conflict with John over her treatment gives shape to the wallpaper's personality:

It is so discouraging not to have any advice and companionship about my work. When I get really well, John says we will ask Cousin Henry and Julia down for a long visit; but he says he would as soon put fireworks in my pillow-case as to let me have those stimulating people about now.

I wish I could get well faster.

But I must not think about that. This paper looks to me as if it knew what a vicious influence it had!

There is a recurrent spot where the patter lolls like a broken neck and two bulbous eyes stare at you upside down. (7)

The wallpaper starts to take on human characteristics, "looking" at the narrator with its staring "bulbous eyes." But what's really animating the wallpaper's "vicious" nature? The narrator's discouragement at her own loneliness and lack of stimulation. And she's pretty clear about the cause: John, who refuses to allow her company she craves in the name of getting the narrator "really well." By placing John's patronizing behavior *right next* to complaints about the wallpaper's vicious character, the narrator is implying criticism of *John's* character — criticisms that she is too well-bred (or repressed) to express openly, even to the "dead paper" of her own journal.

As the narrator sleeps in her nailed-down bed and hides her writing from John and Jennie, we finally start to see the emergence of the creeping woman behind the wallpaper: "I can see a strange, provoking, formless sort of figure, that seems to skulk about behind that silly and conspicuous front design" (8). So, the "front design," the actual squiggles and zigzags of the

wallpaper, now appears to be concealing someone skulking behind, someone "strange" and "provoking." But — isn't the *narrator* kind of strange and provoking? She's definitely annoying John and Jennie with her persistent refusal to get well, and we don't think anyone would argue against "strange."

The narrator has constructed a clever series of parallels between John, the pattern of the paper, and imprisonment — but what is a prison without a prisoner? We know who John's prisoner is (the narrator), but only by implication; the narrator seems unable to articulate her own resentment and claustrophobia directly. Instead, her desperation finds form behind the wallpaper's design, as a "woman stooping down and creeping about behind that paper" (11).

As the narrator grows more and more desperate, she decides that the "dim sub-pattern" (13) is a woman who, by daylight, is "subdued, quiet" (13). This woman's silence, the narrator guesses, comes from being caught in the pattern of the paper, and "it keeps [the narrator] quiet by the hour" (13). As John steps up his campaign to make the narrator rest (driving her to acknowledge that she is "getting a little afraid of John"), the woman in the wallpaper becomes clearer to both the narrator and the reader. The woman is trapped and quiet — by *daylight*, when the narrator is being kept napping against her will, when she wants to be active.

The wallpaper becomes a kind of illness spreading throughout their home: Jennie scolds the narrator for getting yellow stains on all of her clothes and John's, and the narrator observes a curious, musty smell to the paper that "creeps all over the house" (14). Here is the first hint we get that the paper's function as a prison is not limited to the room where the narrator is often trapped; the paper/prison permeates the narrator's environment. While this particular paper may have been the focus of her fantasies, perhaps she would have been no better in a different house, with a different attic room. After all, John is her prison, not the wallpaper.

So, things are definitely coming to a head, and we are aware of this because that woman behind the wallpaper becomes increasingly physical: "the woman behind [the wallpaper] shakes it!" (15), our narrator observes, strengthening the parallel between the paper's pattern and prison bars once again. The woman is "trying to climb through" but the wallpaper "strangles so" (15).

The narrator's identification with the woman behind the wallpaper is pretty much established by now, but Gilman wants to underline and basically surround this idea with stars and exclamation points. Once the narrator informs us that, "I always lock the door when I creep by daylight" (16) we really know things are not all well in Narratorland.

During the day, when she (they?) is (are?) left alone, both the narrator and the woman move silently, secretly about the house — guiltily, for fear of being caught. This need for quiet reminds us of all of those times when the narrator had to hide her writing from John and Jennie for fear that they would scold her; her speculations about the wallpaper become distorted, funhouse mirror versions of the kind of imaginative release the narrator used to get from writing freely. And nighttime appears to be lockdown, for both the narrator and for the woman.

And now, we're at the end! And it's a doozy: the narrator's "I" gives way at last to the "I" of the woman in the wallpaper, who comes out of the wallpaper and observes, "It is so pleasant to be

out in this great room and creep around as I please!" (18). Ruh roh!

Gilman has carefully built the foundation of this complete submersion of the narrator into the identity of the creeping woman. Because the narrator is unable to speak about her own imprisonment, the only way that she can express her frustration with her situation is on the slant, with pity and horror for the woman behind the bars of the wallpaper pattern. Because the narrator has no means to free herself from her submissive relationship with John, she finds a kind of liberty in tearing at the wallpaper to release her counterpart in the walls.

By submerging herself in the woman behind the wallpaper — and by giving herself completely over to madness — the narrator manages (in a kind of negative, unfortunate way) to defeat John. She's "'got out at last […] in spite of you and Jane'" (19), the creeping woman tells John triumphantly. How can John, as a physician dismiss her symptoms now? How can he belittle the seriousness of the narrator/woman's condition as she's creeping "smoothly on the floor" (18)? She has, at last, proved all his patronizing dismissals of her fears about her emotional state wrong — but at the cost of her own sanity.

But could she be real?
OK, so, there's plenty of evidence in the text that the narrator's illness and frustration drives her to create a second version of herself (the woman in the wallpaper) as an expression of negative feeling that she can't otherwise express. Probably, there isn't really a woman in the wallpaper with a burning desire to possess unsuspecting women. However, the mounting sense of claustrophobia and suspense in "The Yellow Wallpaper" could also make this work as a straight tale of supernatural horror. We've even seen "The Yellow Wallpaper" published in some anthologies of horror stories.

Why push the madness angle? The thing is — pretty much all horror is really about some other social anxiety. Like, zombies in that movie *Dawn of the Dead* might represent concerns about mob action and mass culture. Slasher movies like the *Friday the 13th* and *Halloween* franchises do seem to be about punishing teen sexuality. And one popular reading of *Dracula* is that Bram Stoker is making real blood-suckers out of the metaphorical exploitation of the lower classes by the old European aristocracy.

So, "The Yellow Wallpaper" works as both horror (we totally shuddered when the woman finally appears in the flesh at the end, there) and as social commentary — just as the woman behind the wallpaper works as both a literal monster and figurative projection of the narrator's own repressed rage.

Mary Character Analysis

A woman who takes care of the newborn. Use of the name "Mary" conjures up the idea of the iconic Virgin Mary.

Jennie Character Analysis

John's sister who happily assumes all the traditional duties of a housewife so the narrator is free to sit in her room all day.

Character Roles

Protagonist
The Narrator
We're privy only to the narrator's thoughts, and it's clear that she's the central figure in the story. Since we see only her conflicts and problems, she's the character that we root for. She also undergoes more character transformations than anyone else in the story. For instance, she simultaneously goes from submissive to assertive and from sane to insane. Everyone else stays relatively constant.

Antagonist
John, and the rest of patriarchal society
On the face of it, John is the primary obstacle standing in the way of the narrator's desires to pick her own bedroom, spend her time writing, and hang out with friends. He tells her where to sleep, what medicines to take, whom she can hang out with, and even whether her health is improving. To pin John down as the bad guy, however, would be to miss an important component of the story. The narrator's brother holds many of the same opinions as John, and one of the narrator's female friends also receives poor medical treatment at the hands of a male doctor. To shorten matters, although John may represent the greatest antagonist within this story, he serves as an embodiment of greater antagonistic societal forces.

Foil
The Narrator and Jennie
Jennie is content to spend her time as a perfect housewife; she is upheld as the ideal of femininity in the story, while the narrator is portrayed as strange for desiring to write. Jennie, being the perfect woman of the time, expresses her confusion as to why the narrator would enjoy writing.

Character Clues

Occupation
Both the narrator's husband and her brother are physicians, corroborating the idea that men in the story enjoy greater freedom of movement and more fulfilling work lives. The narrator is prevented from being either a housewife or mother, as other, more appropriate women fill those roles. With the exception of the narrator, then, everyone tends to be the stereotypical embodiment of her occupation. The doctors are rational and frown on superstition. The nanny and the housekeeper are nurturing and refuse to look beyond their assigned societal roles. Only our narrator, who lacks a truly accepted occupation, has undefined character traits. She's at

first the submissive and proper wife, but this soon gives way to rather different characteristics.

Names

The most significant name in the story is, in fact, the narrator's *lack* of a name. Really, who doesn't name the central narrator of a story? (Ralph Ellison in *Invisible Man*, for one.) When it happens, this deliberate omission can actually draw greater attention to the narrator and can elicit all sorts of interesting speculation as to why he/she doesn't have a name. In *Invisible Man*, the narrator is meant to speak in a disembodied voice. In "The Yellow Wallpaper," the narrator serves a similar function, as a disembodied voice speaking for a collective. More pertinent to the story's feminist undertones, though, is the idea that the narrator is defined only in relation to her husband. She lacks a concrete identity of her own.

Wait. There's this quote here: "'I've got out at last,' said I, 'in spite of you and Jane. And I've pulled off most of the paper, so you can't put me back!'" Are you thinking what we're thinking? *Who the heck is Jane?* Scholars have argued that Jane is actually the name of the narrator. Other scholars argue that "Jane" is simply a typo. Since the typo argument is a way less nuanced and interesting, let's talk about this Jane business. When the narrator says she's been freed "in spite of you and Jane," we might understand her to admit to her own complicity in being trapped and repressed. "Jane" is partly responsible for her own captivity. The name also provides a neat counterpoint to the name "John," which is a nifty literary device.

So who is the narrator really, by the end of the story? A new, liberated woman who's shed the old "Jane" behind? What's in a name anyway?

Literary Devices

Symbols, Imagery, Allegory

The Wallpaper's Pattern

It's definitely not a coincidence that the woman in the wallpaper is trapped behind a pattern. We can conceive of societal norms and mores as types of patterns that metaphorically restrict our movements. The woman whom the narrator imagines she sees trapped behind a pattern is simply a more direct embodiment of that metaphorical restriction.

The Paper

Scholars have made much of the fact that the narrator starts referring to the wallpaper as "the paper." Given that the narrator has a repressed literary bent, it is no great stretch of the imagination to posit that the (wall)paper becomes her text. Her intellect restrained from reading and writing, the narrator's mind instead turns to her surroundings and settles upon the wallpaper as an intellectual challenge.

Moonlight

In "The Yellow Wallpaper," moonlight represents as time for the feminine. During the day, the narrator writes that the woman trapped in the wallpaper is motionless and immobile. As

moonlight strikes the wall, however, the woman begins to move or, perhaps more accurately, to creep. This pattern mirrors the narrator's own daily movements. During the day, she sleeps; at night she lies awake, alert, and invested in the intellectual activity that she must suppress during the day while her husband is watching.

The House
See Setting for a complete discussion.

The Bed
It's big, heavy, and chained down to the floor. Some critics argue this represents repressed female sexuality, probably because a bed is where people have sex, and chains are a repressive measure. We think it's a bit of a stretch, but it's your call.

Setting

Rambling, isolated countryside estate, around 1885.
The tangible setting of "The Yellow Wallpaper" reinforces all of the intangible feelings and the attitudes expressed in the story. What do we mean by this? Let's start with this passage: "[The house] is quite alone standing well back from the road, quite three miles from the village. It makes me think of English places that you read about, for there are hedges and walls and gates that lock, and lots of separate little houses for the gardeners and people." It's a fancy house, yes, but more saliently, it stands back away from the road and contains many "locks" and "separate little houses." Overall, this is a very isolating place. It's separate from the road and therefore, we would argue, separated from society; the house itself is described as a place that binds and restricts. Now think about the narrator's emotional position: isolated and restricted, her emotional position mirrors the house's physical set-up.

Within the house itself, the narrator is primarily confined to a "big, airy room…with windows that look all ways." In keeping with the themes of isolation and restriction, the windows that look out everywhere are *barred*, preventing any sort of escape. The narrator is able to see, but not participate in, what happens outside her room.

There is yet another connection to draw between the narrator and her physical setting, however. Do you notice how John tends to infantilize his wife? Calling her his "blessed little goose" is only the least of it. He treats her more like a child than an adult; it comes as no surprise that the narrator's bedroom used to be…(gasp!) a nursery.

Lastly, don't forget that the story was written in the late 19th century, which anchors it in a very specific historical moment in terms of women and their perceived abilities. Except for the wallpaper madness at the end, the narrator's story would have been rather typical at the time of publication.

Narrator Point of View

First Person (Central Narrator)

This is a tough perspective when the narrator is slowly sinking into madness. Is there really a woman creeping around outside in the bushes? Probably not. Is there really a woman trapped in the wallpaper? Definitely not. But is the pattern of the wallpaper interesting and confusing? Probably yes. The author's use of the first person to convey the story allows readers to go along for the ride into madness and cultivates a certain amount of sympathy for the narrator and her plight. The constant use of "I" puts us right in the narrator's head and allows us to empathize with her.

Genre

Literary Fiction, Gothic or Horror Fiction

Ring the alarm, there's a woman trapped in the wallpaper! Or is that just a figment in the narrator's imagination? When "The Yellow Wallpaper" first came out, the public didn't quite understand the message. The piece was treated as a horror story, kind of like the 19th century equivalent to *The Exorcist*. Nowadays, however, we understand "The Yellow Wallpaper" as an early feminist work.

As we wrote in the "Book," Gilman never intended "The Yellow Wallpaper" to be a Gothic horror, but as a cautionary tale about what supposed rest cures could do to the mental stability of patients. As Gilman stated in "Why I Wrote the *Yellow Wallpaper*," the story "was not intended to drive people crazy, but to save people from being driven crazy, and it worked." As such, we think it always was a work of literary fiction, but that people back in the 19th century just didn't get that.

Tone

Ironic Indirection

If we took the narrator's words at face value, we would believe that her husband is kind and loving, that she really is physically ill, and that women really do get trapped in wallpaper. All of this is questionable at best and mostly dead wrong. This is part of the fun of first person narration – you're never quite sure if the narrator's perceptions actually reflect what's going on. The narrator's tone also clues us into her character – her uncertainty and hesitation at the start of the story, and her determination towards the end.

Writing Style

Slow Descent Into Madness

Over the course of the story, we witness the narrator gradually losing her mind. In the beginning, she can offer calm and logical descriptions of her surroundings. Soon, however, she attempts to have a rational conversation with her husband but ends up crying and pleading. By the end of the story, she is convinced that the wallpaper is moving, as a woman trapped inside attempts to break free. As the story unfolds, however, the prose remains very crisp and factual. We can ascertain the narrator's listlessness as she lies in bed and follows the pattern of the wallpaper. As her delusions increase and she becomes more convinced that a woman is trapped within the paper, the prose becomes more urgent and more secretive.

What's Up With the Title?

The title object refers to the wallpaper in the room where the protagonist spends most of her time. Since she is essentially trapped in her room with nothing to do, she spends her time staring at the pattern of the wallpaper, becoming more and more obsessed with the paper.

What's Up With the Ending?

Ah, endings. Always a tricky business. In "The Yellow Wallpaper," the (by now very mentally ill) narrator has stripped off all the wallpaper in her room and is creeping around when her husband shows up at the door. She tells him that she's free and that she's liberated herself. He faints and she continues to creep around the room.

First of all, this leaves us with a big, huge question that we address in "Themes and Quotes." The question: Is the narrator really liberated? We're inclined towards saying no, given that she's still creeping around the room and that her mind is now insane. How is this freedom?

We next turn our attention to the narrator's husband John. As soon as he sees her, he faints. Some critics have argued that John's faint demonstrates a moment of feminine weakness in the character of the story's otherwise quintessential man. This provides a degree of balance to the story. The narrator attains freedom; John turns into a woman. But that argument depends on your belief that the narrator is actually free at the end. Tricky.

Did You Know?

Trivia

- Charlotte Perkins Gilman sent a copy of "The Yellow Wallpaper" to the physician who had prescribed her a "rest cure." He subsequently altered the way he treated women for depression.

- Gilman divorced her husband Charles Stetson in 1894. Divorce, we might point out, was very rare at this period in time.
- Gilman's second marriage was to her first cousin, George Houghton Gilman.
- Gilman committed suicide in 1935 after being diagnosed with inoperable breast cancer.

Steaminess Rating

G
Clearly the narrator and her husband must have had sex at one point – when the story begins, the narrator has just had a baby. But they don't seem to be having any right now, and sex is definitely not a part of this story, unless you want to be daring and argue that the narrator is portrayed as existing *for* her husband, and this functionality probably extends to his sexual needs as well.

Allusions and Cultural References

Historical References
Weir Mitchell (3.4)

Best of the Web

Movie or TV Productions
The Yellow Wallpaper (1977)
http://www.imdb.com/title/tt0856286/
Short film adaptation produced by Marie Ashton.

The Yellow Wallpaper (1989)
http://www.imdb.com/title/tt0314918/
BBC mini-series directed by John Clive.

The Yellow Wallpaper (2008)
http://www.imdb.com/title/tt0790788/
The storyline of this movie is altered and lengthened so that the narrator believes her dead daughter is the one trapped in the wallpaper.

Audios
Sample from the Audio Book
http://www.audiobooksforfree.com/download/default.asp?refnum=1000449
A sample from the audio book narrated by Margaret Wooster.

Images
Charlotte Perkins Gilman
http://img.tfd.com/authors/gilman.jpg
Photo of the author.

Charlotte Perkins Gilman
http://content.answers.com/main/content/wp/en/thumb/e/eb/200px-Charlotte_Perkins_Gilman_c._1900.jpg
Another photo of the author.

Documents
"Why I Wrote *The Yellow Wallpaper*"
http://www.library.csi.cuny.edu/dept/history/lavender/whyyw.html
An article written by Charlotte Perkins Gilman in 1913.

Websites
The Charlotte Perkins Gilman Society
http://web.cortland.edu/gilman/
An organization dedicated to encouraging an interest in Gilman and her work.

Charlotte Perkins Gilman
http://www.womenwriters.net/domesticgoddess/gilman1.html
A great resource with biography, bibliography, other kinds of –ography, links to critical essays, etc.

Silas Weir Mitchell
http://www.whonamedit.com/doctor.cfm/959.html
A link to information on the physician who treated Gilman and helped inspire "The Yellow Wallpaper."

Printed in Great Britain
by Amazon